On Great Western Lines

Roy Hobbs

First published 2000

ISBN 07110 2757 9

Published by Ian Allan Publishing

An imprint of Ian Allan Ltd, Terminal House, Shepperton, Surrey TW17 8AS; and printed by Ian Allan Printing Ltd., Riverdene Business Park, Hersham, Surrey KT12 4RG.

Code: 0011/B2

Front Cover: 'King' class 4-6-0 No 6010 *King Charles I* heads an unidentified up excursion on 4 November 1961 over the well-known water troughs at Goring, north of Reading, with its tender scoop in operation. *T.B. Owen*

Rear Cover: '14xx' class 0-4-2T No 1421 approaches the curve marking the entry to Bourne End station on the final lap of its journey from Marlow on 8 July 1962. The branch still remains operational, but has been reduced to 'basic railway' standards, the original distinctive station terminal building having long since been demolished.

This Page: In an unlikely role, and bearing an official headboard, Churchward '47xx' class 2-8-0 No 4704 passes the Ranelagh Bridge stabling point shortly after leaving Paddington with the down 'Royal Duchy' on 16 August 1958. *R.C. Riley*

All uncredited photos taken by the author.

Introduction

What was it that made the Great Western, in particular, such a distinctive and popular system to so many enthusiasts and the public at large? One can only assume that this arose mainly from the Company's early appreciation of good marketing and publicity, as evidenced by their early entry into this particular field. After 1923 and especially in the 1930s, they became a major publisher in their own right, producing books, jigsaw puzzles, postcards, etc. Apart from the well known *Holiday Haunts* publication (first published in 1906), promoting their own holiday resorts, the enthusiast was also catered for by the 'GWR Engines' series, first appearing in a slightly different guise in 1911.

The majority of the Company's engines also possessed a uniquely distinctive appearance and character, which had continued under the reign of successive Chief Engineers from around the late 19th century until Nationalisation. All this gave it the advantage of possessing what is known in current jargon as a particular corporate image, being readily identifiable in overall style and design standards.

My own introduction to an interest in railways and the GWR was towards the end of the last war, when I was evacuated to Somerset from my Surrey home. This saw my being billeted in Langport with, fortuitously, the Castle Cary to Taunton main line located at the end of the garden! The longer passenger trains during this wartime period were often double-headed in an easterly direction by one of Taunton's 'Bulldog' class 4-4-0s, either No 3443 *Chaffinch* or No 3444 *Cormorant*, to assist over Savernake bank. I developed a particular affection for this class, and it is to my regret that none survived long enough to be preserved. These experiences led to my having a particular liking for the GWR and its Swindon products, this being reinforced by periodic visits to my grandmother's Exeter home.

In preparing this volume and taking into account the various albums already devoted to the Company and its Western Region successor, an attempt has been made to cover areas not largely dealt with previously. Obviously, with this fairly extensive system there are bound to be omissions, but I have endeavoured to provide a balanced coverage of the various loco classes and lines operated from the mid-1950s until the end of steam. Historical information is, of necessity, restricted, and for further detail the reader is referred to the many excellent publications which already exist, some being listed below.

Picture order has been determined by starting from Paddington, and following those lines and branches to the South and West of England, then broadly tracing routes through the Southern Midlands and Welsh Border counties. We then travel via Swindon and Bristol into Southern Wales, and head north into Cambrian Railways territory. Our steps are then retraced and continue from London northwards, via the Birmingham main line and Shrewsbury to the Wrexham area.

Bibliography

Baker: *Rail Atlas Great Britain & Ireland;* OPC

W. Philip Connolly: *British Railways Pre-grouping Atlas & Gazetteer;* Ian Allan.

G. Daniels & L.A. Dench: *Passengers No More (3rd Edition);* Ian Allan.

Grey: *Great Loco Story;* Quadrant

Lewthwaite: *Branch Line Index (2nd Edition);* Branch Line Society

McDermot: *History of the Great Western Railway (Vols 1 & 2)*

Page: *Forgotten Railways: South Wales;* David & Charles

Page: *Rails in the Valleys;* David & Charles

Whitehurst: *Great Western Engines, Names, Numbers, Types and Classes;* OPC

Whitehouse & Thomas: *The Great Western Railway: 150 Glorious Years;* David & Charles

Various authors: *Regional History of the Railways of Great Britain (Vols. 1,7,11,12 & 13);* David & Charles

Society Journals : LCGB Bulletin, Railway Observer (RCTS). SLS Journal

Magazines: *Great Western Journal, Railway Magazine, Steam World, Trains Illustrated*

Acknowledgements

This book could not have been completed without the assistance of many talented photographers, to whom I offer my grateful thanks for the use of their now valuable transparencies. For their help with regard to various queries and other matters, I would especially mention Alan Jarvis and Eric Youldon, whose co-operation is much appreciated. The Railway Studies Library of Devon County Council, located at Newton Abbot, has also provided a useful source of reference, and is readily recommended to other researchers into the subject.

Roy Hobbs
Exeter
Devon

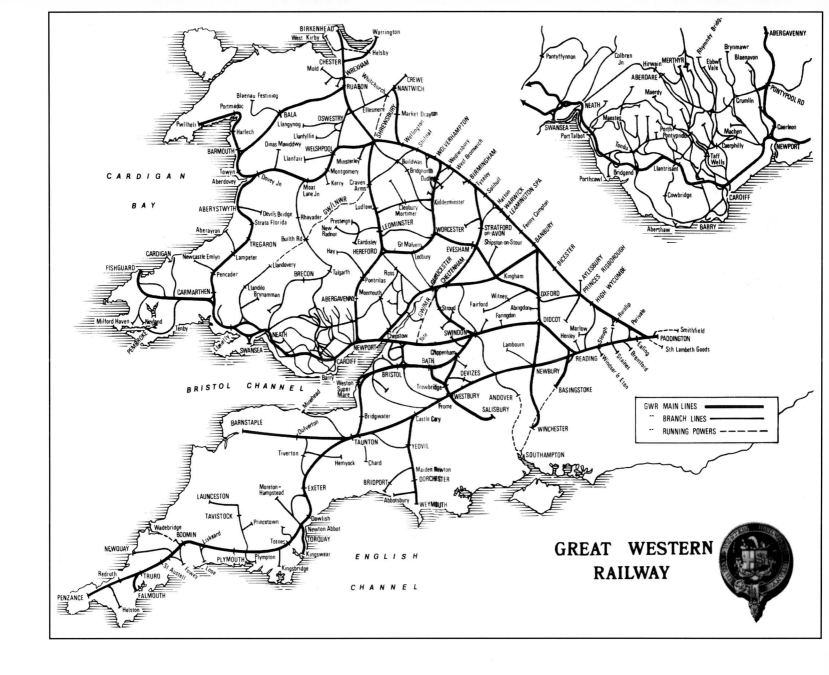

GREAT WESTERN
RAILWAY

GWR MAIN LINES	▬▬▬▬
BRANCH LINES	───
RUNNING POWERS	─ ─ ─

Above: The empty coaching stock workings between Old Oak Common and Paddington were, for many years, handled by the various types of 0-6-0PT, including the '15xx', '57xx' and '94xx' classes. Illustrated in this view taken from the train, '94xx' class locomotive No 9495 is approaching Royal Oak station outside Paddington on 22 June 1963 with a rake of carriages painted in the chocolate and cream colours of the Region and its predecessor, rather than the BR standard lined maroon livery then in general use for main line stock. During the late 1950s there was a certain amount of regional autonomy, and the decision was taken to paint locos, together with rolling stock, used on the principal named trains in the traditional colours of the old Company.

Right: Along the Maidenhead to High Wycombe line we see a distant view of '14xx' class 0-4-2T No 1421 with its single autocoach. shortly after leaving Cookham and against the backdrop of the Chiltern Hills, as it descends the line to Bourne End with its working to Marlow on 8 July 1962. The section north of Bourne End was closed to all traffic on 4 May 1970.

Left: Bourne End station (Marlow Road until 1874), located on the Maidenhead to High Wycombe line, was opened by the Wycombe Railway on 1 August 1854, being constructed initially to broad gauge. This included the building of two timber viaducts in the vicinity; one over the Thames and another over Cock Marsh meadow. Conversion to standard gauge took place in 1870. Bourne End formed the junction for the Marlow branch, the local train later being popularly identified as the 'Marlow Donkey'. The Great Marlow Railway Company had been formed in 1868 by a group of local businessmen, the almost 3 mile branch being opened to traffic on 28 June 1873. On the final day of steam working, as the previous photograph, No 1421 is viewed through the station footbridge as it departs for Cookham.

Above: During the Christmas period many additional trains are run to cater for the vastly increased postal traffic which occurs at this time. A westbound van train is illustrated, with 'Hall' class 4-6-0 No 6933 *Birtles Hall*, approaching Southcote Junction west of Reading on 21 December 1963. The Basingstoke and West of England lines diverged here, along with the line to Reading Central Goods (otherwise the Coley branch).

The Didcot, Newbury and Southampton Railway was incorporated on 5 August 1873, the initial Didcot to Newbury section being opened as a single line on 13 April 1882 and worked by the GWR from the outset. Early intentions were to operate via Whitchurch and Micheldever, these plans being abandoned in an 1882 Act, and replaced with a route via Winchester. This single line section was opened to passengers on 4 May 1885. It proved impossible to raise sufficient capital for completion through to Southampton, so agreement was reached with the LSWR for a connection from Winchester to their line at Shawford Junction, provided the latter had operational powers to Winchester as an interchange point. This final link was opened on 1 October 1891, the Company having earlier renounced all rights for a separate line into Southampton. Some GWR trains later ran throughout, by agreement only, rather than with running powers. Churn station, its island platform nestling in the Berkshire Downs, must have been one of the most primitive and isolated halts on the system, as illustrated by this view of '43xx' class 2-6-0 No 6333 departing with a Newbury bound train on 27 February 1960. Access was extremely limited, being mainly by tracks and footpaths across the downs. Opened on 6 July 1888, it had been constructed to serve the nearby rifle ranges together with annual camps. Due to increased military traffic in World War II, the whole route was upgraded, line doubling taking place between Didcot and Newbury and from Enborne Junction to Woodhay. Crossing loops were added, existing ones extended, and a spur built from Worthy Down to the up Southern Railway main line at Winchester Junction. Final freight closure came in April 1966. *T.B. Owen*

This rare colour view, taken on the Lambourn branch, shows the terminus with Class 57xx 0-6-0PT No 4609 about to depart for Newbury with a morning train on 28 April 1959. The line was opened on 2 April 1898, and eventually closed to passengers on 4 January 1960. Part of the line was retained for freight to serve the RNAD Ordnance Depot at Welford Park, this having its own long siding and small diesel locomotive, but maintenance costs brought abandonment in June 1972. Lambourn was the home of various well-known racing stables, and considerable revenue was derived from this traffic, amounting at one time to some 1,000 movements annually. The line was used for railcar experiments in 1937, and No 18 was strengthened especially for trailer use, two horseboxes being permanently allocated to enable mixed working. Interesting motive power to work the branch included, during the late 1930s, the last two Wolverhampton-built Class 850 0-6-0STs Nos 1925 and 2007. The three ex-Midland & South Western Junction Railway (M&SWJR) Class 13xx 2-4-0s were also located here for many years. *Alan Jarvis*

WHISTLE

Left: The town of Marlborough in Wiltshire was, at one time, in the position of being served by two separate systems, those of the M&SWJR and the GWR. These were ultimately rationalised following the 1923 grouping, the GWR station closing to passengers on 6 March 1933, but retained for freight. In 1873 the M&SWJR were given running powers over the GWR section to Savernake, but the latter proved extremely obstructive, often using dubious methods to hold trains at Savernake for lengthy periods before they could continue forward. This resulted in the M&SWJR constructing a separate line in 1898 to bypass the GWR route from just north of Marlborough to its own southern section between Savernake (Grafton Junction) and Andover (Red Post Junction). Class 57xx 0-6-0PT No 9672 is seen here on a local working at the former M&SWJR station on 15 March 1958. *T.B. Owen*

Above: A nicely prepared 'Modified Hall' class 4-6-0 No 6963, formerly *Throwley Hall* (until nameplate removal), works the Locomotive Club of Great Britain 'Wessex Downsman' railtour of 4 April 1965 past Bromham & Rowde Halt on the line from Patney & Chirton to Holt Junction via Devizes. Despite apparent complete closure taking place on 18 April 1966, the line briefly came into its own again in June 1966, the Royal Train stabling east of Holt for the night.

11

Above: Having its tanks replenished at Radstock West, '57xx' class 0-6-0PT No 9615 is shown heading a Bristol to Frome train on 22 August 1959. The line was closed to passenger operation on 2 November 1959. Following this date, however, it remained open from Frome to Radstock in order to serve a wagon works and ARC Whatley Quarry, before being cut back to Hapsford (Somerset Quarry Junction). *Alan Jarvis*

Right: Swindon built Standard Class 3MT 2-6-2T No 82042 makes its way along the short connecting line, now a public footpath, between Yeovil Town and Yeovil (Pen Mill) in May 1964 with the shortly-to-be withdrawn service from Taunton. This class, although built in the post-Nationalisation era, was basically a Swindon design and embodied a modified Swindon No 2 boiler incorporating a dome and normal superheater. This section of line originated as the result of extending from the Bristol & Exeter broad gauge terminus at Hendford on 2 February 1857, Yeovil Town opening on 1 June 1861. Mixed gauge was employed from 12 November 1868, full conversion taking place on 30 June 1879. Passenger working ceased on 29 November 1965, freight surviving to Hendford goods until 6 November 1968.

Left: The line from Dorchester Junction to Weymouth, through GWR territory, was operated jointly with the London & South Western Railway (later SR). On 17 September 1962 'Grange' class 4-6-0 No 6835 *Eastham Grange* departs Weymouth for Bristol, whilst Giesl ejector fitted 'Bulleid Pacific' No 34064 *Fighter Command* waits with its Waterloo duty. *Alan Jarvis*

Above: Boat trains from London for the Channel Islands, on arriving at Weymouth, were conveyed over the last 1¼ mile section to the dockside on the roadside Weymouth Quay tramway. This left the main line at Weymouth Junction, just north of the terminus, where during the 1950s the train was taken forward by one of the six '1366' class outside-cylindered

0-6-0PTs. Seen on the last stage of this journey on 11 September 1959 No 1371, built 1934 and one of two withdrawn in 1960, is seen threading its way between the various parked cars which, as today, show little regard for admonishments on adjacent buildings. *Alan Jarvis*

Heading a Yeovil Town to Taunton train 'Small Prairie' 2-6-2T No 4569 is seen near Langport in May 1964 crossing the River Parrett with Muchelney church in the background. The broad gauge line from Durston to Hendford was opened on 1 October 1853 by the Bristol & Exeter Railway, being subsequently converted to mixed gauge in November 1867 as far as Yeovil Town, and then standard gauge on 30 June 1879. During World War II one of the return services to Taunton was worked by an SR loco, usually a 'T9', and men in order to provide route knowledge for possible wartime emergency working. This duty ceased in 1945, but came of use in September 1946 when, due to flooding at Seaton Junction and Broad Clyst, several services on the SR were diverted via Taunton in the up direction. Line closure to all traffic between Hendford and Curry Rivel took effect in July 1964.

Making a spirited departure from Langport East station '51xx' class 2-6-2T No 4143 is depicted heading a Taunton to Castle Cary local working in July 1962. In earlier years this service was operated by one of the GWR auto sets, often hauled by a Westbury '54xx' class 0-6-0PT. The route, which opened throughout on 2 July 1906, involved much heavy engineering, including the ten arch Langport Viaduct with foundations sunk 50ft below the peat of the Somerset Levels flood plain.

Below: Traversing the well-known Tone Viaduct near Venn Cross, Collett '2251' class 0-6-0 No 3205 is seen heading for Taunton with the RCTS/PRC 'Exmoor Ranger' railtour of 27 March 1965. No 3205 is the sole preserved example of its class.

Right: With an interested observer waiting by the foot crossing at Tiverton Junction station on 15 June 1962, a commendably clean 'Hall' class 4-6-0 No 4932 *Hatherton Hall* heads through with a down freight, including permanent way equipment. This was the

point at which branches for its namesake town and that of Hemyock originated, passenger services to the former ceasing on 5 October 1964 and to Hemyock on 9 September 1963. The station closed on 3 March 1986 when Tiverton Parkway opened. *R.C. Riley*

In an unlikely situation heading a rake of coaching stock and bearing express headlamps, '2884' class 2-8-0 No 2887 is seen on 3 May 1964 leaving Exeter St Davids yard with stock forming the RCTS/PRC 'Cornubian' railtour to commemorate the end of steam traction along the main line through Cornwall. The yard has undergone considerable changes since this photograph, the sidings are somewhat reduced. Whilst two roads of the original four road engine shed, hidden behind the loco, have been reinstated and now service local DMU stock.

Launceston station was the meeting point for the LSWR line from Halwill Junction to Wadebridge and Padstow, and the GWR branch from Plymouth.

Depicted here '4575' class 2-6-2T No 5569 has just arrived from the latter on a sunny day in July 1961. Branch passenger closure came about on 31 December 1962, coinciding with the worst blizzards in the area for many years, the last trains being unable to run and the previous two having to be abandoned along the route.

21

Left: The GWR installed water troughs at various sites across the system, to enable through running of the various long distance expresses operated by the Company. One of the better known of these was at Goring-on-Thames, between Reading and Didcot, where 'Hall' class 4-6-0 No 5931 *Hatherley Hall* is illustrated on an up semi-fast on 4 November 1961. *T.B. Owen*

Above: Also seen passing over Goring troughs, on the same day as the opposite view, is '61xx' class 2-6-2T No 6109 with an unidentified up van train. The '61xx' series were a variant of the '51xx' class with increased boiler pressure, being specifically developed in 1931 for London suburban and commuter traffic. With the onset of dieselisation several were transferred away, and could be found at various locations across the

system by the early 1960s. In January 1932 No 6116 was sent to Swindon and fitted with driving wheels of 5ft 3in diameter, in order to establish whether greater acceleration in service could be achieved. The trials were successful, and although no further conversions were undertaken, useful prototype experience was gained for the 1938 81xx series rebuilds, these incorporating 5ft 6in diameter wheels. *T.B.Owen*

The construction of the Fairford branch arose out of a proposal for a railway line between Yarnton and Witney, the Witney Railway Act receiving Royal Assent on 1 August 1859. The line opened on 14 November 1861 for the carriage of passengers and coal, but not for general goods until 1 March 1862, as warehousing was incomplete. From 1 August 1863 the line came under the control of the GWR, taking over from the West Midland Railway, till then responsible for operation. On 29 July 1864 the East Gloucestershire Railway Act was passed, authorising a line between Witney and Cheltenham, this opening as far as Fairford on 15 January 1873. Disputes between the GWR and the Midland Railway in the intervening years, regarding its route and operation had delayed completion, along with considerable difficulty in obtaining financial backing. The EGR along with the Witney Railway was eventually absorbed by the GWR on 1 July 1890. With the continuing lack of financial interest extension plans were finally abandoned, resulting in the line ending in a meadow, ¼ mile beyond Fairford, at which were located the engine shed, turntable and small goods shed. In World War II Carterton station was built to serve nearby Brize Norton aerodrome, special arrangements existing between Brize Norton box and the aerodrome to control aircraft movements across the line in the vicinity. Here '74xx' class 0-6-0PT No 7443 is seen at the terminus in September 1960. Closing to passengers from 18 June 1962, freight operated to Witney until 2 November 1970. *Alan Jarvis*

After the proposal of several abortive schemes in the 1860s, plans were formulated in 1873 for the Banbury & Cheltenham Direct Railway with the intention of connecting 'London and the Midlands and Eastern County Districts by a shorter and more direct route with the South Wales Coalfield and the West of England'. Ironstone deposits in the neighbourhood of Adderbury had been a primary reason for the development of this route, as it was anticipated that some 10,000 tons would be carried daily. The line had origins in a branch connecting Kingham with Chipping Norton, opened in August 1855. An additional section was completed from Kingham to Bourton in 1862, the route subsequently opening throughout in 1906. From May 1906 till September 1939 a regular weekday express operated to and from Cardiff and Newcastle, initially 'Castle' hauled, whilst through coaches to and from Cheltenham and London also ran. By the late 1950s only an infrequent local service operated. Class 4575 2-6-2T No 5514 is seen departing from Notgrove with a Kingham train on 25 July 1959. Passenger services from Kingham to Cheltenham ceased on 15 October 1962, freight traffic between Kingham and Bourton lasting until September 1964. *T.B. Owen*

Left: Bearley was situated on a triangular junction, where the Alcester (Midland Railway) to Hatton line crossed that from Stratford-on-Avon to Birmingham via Henley-in-Arden. The 6.32pm train from Leamington Spa to Stratford is shown passing the station in low evening light on 28 May 1957, with '58xx' class 0-4-2T No 5813, still displaying 'GWR' on the tank side nine years after Nationalisation. *John Edgington*

Below: On 19 September 1965 restored '45xx' class 2-6-2T No 4555 and '14xx' class 0-4-2T No 1420 doublehead what was then believed to be a final steam passenger working over the Severn Valley line from Bewdley to Alveley Colliery. The train is shown passing Arley on the outward journey, which is in complete contrast to its current pristine state under Severn Valley Railway (SVR) ownership, with the removed running line now replaced along with various sidings. BR passenger services from Bewdley to Shrewsbury ended on 9 September 1963 when the line was cut back to Alveley Colliery, final closure being on 3 May 1970. Initial reopening by the SVR from Bridgnorth to Hampton Loade was on 23 June 1970, the line now having reached its intended terminus at Kidderminster.

During the period under review the Stephenson Locomotive Society (Birmingham Area) organised several last runs for especially notable locomotive classes, an early example running from Birmingham to Swindon hauled by the last 'Bulldog' class 4-4-0 No 3454 *Skylark* in June 1951. During April 1963 'King' class 4-6-0 No 6018 *King Henry VI*, withdrawn in December 1962, was specially reinstated for a similar run to Swindon, travelling outward via the Paddington main line and Greenford loop. In this instance, the last 'County' class 4-6-0 No 1011 *County of Chester* is seen leaving Didcot West Curve, returning to Birmingham from Swindon on 20 September 1964. This class, despite higher boiler pressure and smaller diameter wheels, producing a nominally higher tractive effort than a 'Castle', was found inferior in performance, and with two cylinders gave a ride noticeably less smooth than the four cylinder engine.

Another view here of a '47xx' class 2-8-0, on this occasion No 4705, seen on a running-in turn at Challow on 13 May 1961 with a Didcot to Swindon local duty, following completion of overhaul at Swindon Works. These services were regularly used for such purposes, and a variety of large passenger engines could often be found incongruously heading trains of just two coaches! Introduced in 1919, these handsome engines were designed specifically for fast freight working, mostly running overnight, but on summer Saturdays regularly headed relief passenger trains, mainly to the West Country. To the great regret of many enthusiasts none survived long enough to enter preservation, the entire class of nine locos having been withdrawn by May 1964. *R.C. Riley*

Left: In view of its rarity the author is especially pleased to include this fine study of former M&SWJR 2-4-0 No 1336, built by Dubs in 1894, departing Cirencester (Watermoor) with a Gloucestershire Railway Society special on 9 May 1953. This engine, originally M&SWJR No 12, was withdrawn the following year, being the last survivor of three sister engines, the others having been taken out of service in 1952. The class was for many years particularly associated with the Lambourn branch, on which they operated for until withdrawal, being replaced initially by Dean Goods 0-6-0s. They were the last representatives of this particular subsidiary, absorbed at the 1923 grouping. *J.M. Jarvis*

Above: Towards the end of the well-known auto service, run between Gloucester and Chalford, engines other than the usual auto-fitted '14xx' class 0-4-2Ts were often employed. '57xx' class 0-6-0PT No 3681 is here approaching Chalford, in September 1964, where it would be required to run round, due to the lack of appropriate equipment for auto working.

A Chalford bound auto train is seen here heading along the Golden Valley near Brimscombe Bridge Halt in June 1964, comprising '14xx' class 0-4-2T No 1472 and its solitary auto coach, before services ended on 2 November 1964. An earlier attempt to end their operation had been proposed in Spring 1962, but was rejected by the local Transport User's Consultative Committee (TUCC). A subsequent proposal was accepted, however, and shortly after closure the demolition of Brimscombe's fine Cotswold stone station provided their final epitaph.

32

Barbers Bridge station on the Gloucester to Ledbury branch is the location of this view, with '64xx' class 0-6-0PT No 6424 arriving on 23 June 1962, some three years after passenger closure, with a Gloucestershire Railway Society special train. As shown by the general state of the station area, nature is already taking hold following passenger withdrawal. Before the 1907 opening of the North Warwickshire line this provided the shortest route between Birmingham and Gloucester. Passenger services ceased on 13 July 1959, Ledbury to Dymock closing to all traffic. *Roy Denison*

Above: The route from Cheltenham to Stratford-on-Avon via Honeybourne was completed on 1 August 1899. Illustrated with one of the auto trains serving local stations is '14xx' class 0-4-2T No 1424 departing Broadway on 27 February 1960. This particular service between Cheltenham and Honeybourne ended on 7 March 1960, whilst that from Honeybourne to Stratford lasted until 5 May 1969. The line continued as a through passenger route until 25 March 1968, the last single railcar service running between Gloucester and Leamington Spa. Operation for freight remained up to 1976, when a serious derailment near Winchcombe preceded complete closure. Fortunately, the Toddington to Cheltenham trackbed is now in the care of preservationists, with track being restored westwards to Cheltenham Racecourse. *Gerald Daniels*

Right: An overall view of the system would be incomplete without reference to Swindon Works. Featured here is 'Modified Hall' class 4-6-0 No 6967 *Willesley Hall* standing in the works yard on 5 April 1964 following overhaul. The 'Modified Halls' ('6959' class), an upgraded version of the original '49xx' series, eventually totalled 71 engines, the final example being produced under BR auspices in 1950.

Left: Another loco which passed through Swindon, towards the end of steam working was 'Grange' class 4-6-0 No 6853 *Morehampton Grange*, seen here standing by the turntable adjacent to the Erecting Shop on 16 August 1964. The class was introduced in 1936 with the intention of replacing the ageing '43xx' class 2-6-0s, and incorporated parts from earlier examples, especially wheels and motion. They were designed particularly for fast freight and intermediate passenger working, a total of 80 being built up to 1939. Regrettably, no example survived from this series of engines, none having been fortunate enough to enter the Barry Valhalla at the close of steam operation. However, a project is currently in progress by interested enthusiasts to produce a completely new engine to this design, No 6880 *Betton Grange*.

Above: Almost certainly the final '56xx' class 0-6-2T to be overhauled, No 5691 is depicted on 5 April 1964 in the famous Swindon 'A' Erecting Shop, regrettably now demolished. This type was more usually dealt with in the Caerphilly workshops of the former Rhymney Railway until their closure in 1963, and until early 1962, would have been completed in lined-out green livery before being returned to service.

Below: Getting to grips with a westbound freight 'Modified Hall' class 4-6-0 No 7907 *Hart Hall*, built in the BR era, is seen near Bedminster, south of Bristol, on 19 October 1963. The city tower blocks can just be discerned in the distance. *John Wiltshire Right:*

The county town of Monmouth was the hub of a number of lines, radiating to Pontypool Road, Chepstow, Coleford and Ross-on-Wye. These were progressively closed over several years, services to Ross and Chepstow finishing from 5 January 1959. With BR built autocoach W237W trailing, '14xx' class 0-4-2T No 1455 departs Monmouth (Troy) for Ross-on-Wye on 28 May 1958. During this final period, GWR design railcars operated the remaining services to Pontypool Road and Chepstow. *T.B. Owen*

Although Cinderford (Severn &Wye/Great Western Joint) station had lost its passenger services as far back as November 1958, it still remained in much the same condition when visited by the REC 'Severn Boar' brake van tour, hauled by '16xx' class 0-6-0PT No 1658, more than five years later. This club had organised an imaginative tour of those Forest of Dean lines still open on 20 June 1964. The Severn and Wye Railway had its origins in the Lydney and Lidbrook Railway Co, which had constructed a horse tramway and branches in 1812, and the line from Lydney to Speech House Road entailed the conversion of several of these early tramroads, first opening on the broad gauge on 19 April 1869. Absorption by the Midland and Great Western Railways on 1 July 1894 followed financial difficulties, the locomotive stock being split between the two systems.

This view depicts No 1658 at the end of the Northern United Colliery branch, one of many spurs retained to serve the various mine workings that existed within the Forest. These lines had a special character all their own, which I think is captured here. On the associated GWR section from Bullo Pill it had been planned to make a connection with their Grange Court to Hereford line. However, although completed throughout, freight traffic ended at Drybrook Quarry, whilst a passenger operation from Newnham, initially using steam railcars, ran as far as Drybrook Halt commencing on 4 November 1907. This finished on 7 July 1930, and the last section of nearly three miles through the 638yd Euroclydon Tunnel, though maintained, remained unused until track lifting in January 1917.

Left: An earlier railtour in the Forest of Dean had been run by the REC on 20 April 1958, entitled the 'Severn Rambler'. '54xx' class 0-6-0PT No 5417 is shown leaving Coleford Branch Junction on its way to the Cinderford (Northern United Colliery) branch, later visiting Coleford, which witnessed a passenger train for the first time since 1935. This latter line was especially notable, amongst the Forest railways, for its severe 1 in 30 ruling gradient, local iron ore deposits having been the prime reason for its construction. The '54xx' class locos were particularly distinctive, as compared to their '64xx' and '74xx' sisters, by possessing driving wheels of 5ft 2in diameter, all being designed for local passenger and branch use. *R.C. Riley*

Above: A view here along the Grange Court to Hereford line, with '51xx' class 2-6-2T No 4161 departing Blaisdon Halt with a Hereford working in September 1964, shortly before closure on 2 November 1964. This route was often used by diverted North to West expresses on Sundays, when the Severn Tunnel came under maintenance.

43

Above: Ross-on-Wye was the main intermediate station between Gloucester and Hereford. Collett '2251' class 0-6-0 No 2242 (built 1945) approaches the station on 4 June 1962 with the 4.25pm from Hereford, whilst '51xx' class 2-6-2T No 4135 waits with a working from Gloucester. The station design lives on, being used for that built at Kidderminster on the SVR. *John Wiltshire*

Right: A further view here of a Hereford to Gloucester branch service with '43xx' class 2-6-0 No 7335 departing Hereford, past Ayleston Hill signalbox, with the 2.30pm for Gloucester on 4 October 1962. This particular locomotive was from a later batch of the series, built in 1932. Apart from updating with a side window cab, it had previously been weighted on the front to reduce excessive wear on the leading driving wheels, and numbered in the '93xx' series. These weights were removed in the late 1950s, when its current number was allocated, having previously been identified as No 9313. An example, No 7325, is preserved on the SVR, being rescued from Barry scrapyard in August 1975. *John Wiltshire*

Newport was an important point on the GWR system, being the junction for a number of lines originating in the South Wales coalfield, and provided an important route to the north and Midlands areas via Hereford and Shrewsbury. The final link to Newport (High Street) was initiated by the Pontypool, Caerleon & Newport Railway (PC&NR), incorporated 5 July 1865, to provide a 12 mile route from Pontypool Road, joining the South Wales main line at Maindee (East and West Junctions). The GWR quickly assumed direction of the company, the line opening on 17 September 1874 to goods traffic, replacing the original Monmouthshire Railway route to Newport (Mill Street). With the opening of the Severn Tunnel a direct route was now provided from such places as Southampton in the south to the Midlands and northernmost regions of Britain. '2884' class 2-8-0 No 3810 passes through with a westbound mixed freight on 3 November 1962.
John Wiltshire

Pandy, on the stretch of line between Pontrilas and Abergavenny, is the location of this view showing 'Hall' class 4-6-0 No 6953 *Leighton Hall* with a southbound parcels train on 16 May 1964. The engine's original tender has been replaced by one of later Hawksworth pattern. This section of the North and West route was completed by the Newport, Abergavenny and Hereford Railway, incorporated 3 August 1846, to a point 1mile south of Pontypool, near Coedygric Farm, on 2 January 1854, forming a junction with the Monmouthshire Railway line to Newport. Resulting from earlier agreements, both the London & North Western Railway (LNWR) and GWR inherited running powers, the former commencing services from Hereford on 1 September 1862. Following the opening of the PC&NR route to Newport the LNWR inaugurated a Shrewsbury to Newport (Mill Street) service on 1 January 1875, however, all their passenger workings ceased in March 1879.

John Wiltshire

Left: A nicely cleaned 'Castle' class 4-6-0 No 7023 *Penrice Castle*, built 1949, departs Hereford with the 6.05pm to Paddington on 4 June 1962. The strings of vans in the goods sidings are probably connected with local cider maker Bulmers, who in 1968, were given caretaker status for NRM-owned 'King' class 4-6-0 No 6000 *King George V*, which hauled the first steam railtour in 1971 following the 1968 ban. *John Wiltshire*

Above: A number of branches diverged from the North and West route at Leominster, including the group based on Titley Junction. Amongst these was the branch to Presteigne, just over the Hereford border in Radnorshire. '14xx' class 0-4-2T No 1420 is shown having just arrived with the regular freight duty on 14 September 1964. The Presteigne branch of the Leominster & Kington Railway opened 10 September

1875, both being absorbed by the GWR in 1898. Kington was described in an 1860 guide as 'a favourite starting place for tourists to Aberystwyth, whither a coach runs daily, conveying passengers brought to Kington by railway from Leominster'! Resulting from coal shortages in the 1950s, passenger services were withdrawn on 5 February 1951 with freight lingering on until 28 September 1964. *Roy Denison*

Seen passing Park Junction, Newport on 13 August 1965 with a train of loaded mineral wagons from Newport Docks area is '5205' class 2-8-0T No 5235. The '5205' series was a 1923 development of the earlier '42xx' class with larger cylinders and other minor changes resulting in greater tractive effort, the original design having been introduced by G.J. Churchward in 1910. The only example of this wheel arrangement in the UK, they were produced mainly to meet the needs of the coal traffic in South Wales, where a compact loco with a high adhesive weight was required. Park Junction was the point at which several lines gained access to Newport Docks, and a notable working through here was that of the iron ore trains to Ebbw Vale steelworks. The allocation of BR Standard Class 9F 2-10-0s to these duties in the 1950s eliminated the need for banking, and enabled doubling of loads.

Many locos owned by the GWR and its Western Region successor, were sold on to industrial concerns when no longer required, many being taken by the National Coal Board and predecessors over a number of years following the grouping in 1923. One such example, '57xx' class 0-6-0PT No 7754, is illustrated during October 1969 working their line from Abersychan to Talywain colliery with a train of empty mineral wagons. Originally sold by the Western Region in 1959 to NCB Mountain Ash it kept its identity, and having entered preservation, can now be seen at Llangollen in North Wales.

Below: Approaching Abercynon from the Aberdare direction '56xx' class 0-6-2T No 5692 is seen heading a train of tank wagons for an unknown destination during April 1965. The loco is bearing target H19 signifying '7.05am off Radyr shed, to work as directed by Control'. These targets were used in South Wales to readily identify specific trains, due to the complex nature of coalfield area workings.

Right: Shortly after the end of steam in the Cardiff Valleys, the Swansea Railway Circle organised a commemorative tour of various lines in the area, including a final passenger trip over the short stub that passed across Walnut Tree Viaduct, then serving a local dolomite quarry. The train is shown on its return journey with '56xx' class 0-6-2T No 5643 heading for Penrhos Junction. This viaduct, bridging the Nantgarw

gap south of Taffs Well, was a major engineering landmark in South Wales, comprising a seven-span lattice steel structure 1548ft long and some 120ft above the River Taff. Built for the Barry Railway in 1905, it finally closed on 18 December 1967, but up to 1964 was frequently used by Barry Island excursion traffic; regular summer timetable passenger services ceased in 1935. All but one pier were demolished in 1973.

Left: Situated along the TVR main line between Pontypridd and Abercynon, the sidings by Carn Parc served the local collieries of Abercynon and Lady Windsor, Ynysbwl until all traffic ceased in 1988. '5205' class 2-8-0T No 5206 shunts a train of ICI wagons at this point in April 1965. The Taff Vale Railway was the most significant in South Wales, completing its original main line between Cardiff and Merthyr on 21 April 1841. This first incorporated the use of a rope-worked incline and was superseded in mid-1867 by a conventional line on a 1 in 40 gradient. By the grouping the company embraced a total route mileage of 536 including sidings, achieved both by construction and acquisition of eight independent companies.

Above: In this scene No 5206, shown opposite, is depicted with its return working of laden mineral wagons from Abercynon, passing Machen Quarry on the Brecon & Merthyr (B&M) line from Rhymney. It has just left the B&M Caerphilly branch, and is heading for Bassaleg Junction on the GWR Western Valleys line from Ebbw Vale to Newport.

Close to the village of Pontrhydyfen, and engaged on track lifting duties near Tonmawr Junction on the former Port Talbot Railway system serving Whitworth and Blaenavon collieries, is '94xx' class 0-6-0PT No 9480 seen on 13 August 1965. This had been sold to Swansea breakers in June, and was being operated by contractors responsible for track recovery, including the Rhondda & Swansea Bay (RSB) system, in the locality. Whilst this section had opened on 14 November 1898, specifically for goods and mineral traffic, the PTR had later introduced passenger services, though these were abandoned on 22 September 1930. Final closure to all traffic, including unadvertised miners trains, was on 2 November 1964. The '94xx' class, a tank version of the '2251' series 0-6-0s, introduced in 1947, were built predominantly in the BR era up to 1956. They proved unpopular with crews due to their restricted vision, and were generally outlived by the older '57xx' series.

On that section of line which left the Vale of Neath line at Gelli Tarw Junction towards Merthyr Tydfil, we observe here an auto-train working from Hirwaun for Merthyr propelled by a '64xx' class 0-6-0PT, probably No 6416. This is seen departing the picturesque station of Llwydcoed on 7 July 1962. The remaining intermediate station was Abernant, notable for being originally constructed by Brunel in a florid Italianate manner complete with campaniles, along the style of the first Chippenham station.

The branch, initially broad gauge, was opened on 2 November 1853, taking six years to complete and bankrupting two contractors, mainly due to heavy earthworks in the Taff Valley and building of the Merthyr Tunnel. The original intention was that the line from Neath to Merthyr should be the main route, with a branch to Aberdare. However, the latter was completed first on 24 September 1851, ultimately extending to near Mountain Ash. With the joining of the standard gauge line from Pontypool in April 1864, and the laying of a third rail over the Vale of Neath system, completed the following August, the route to Neath was open throughout. By February 1865 the GWR was in total control, providing it with a lucrative route across some of South Wales richest areas.
Alan Jarvis

Left: The 35 mile long Vale of Neath line between Neath and Pontypool Road, including the famous Crumlin Viaduct, closed throughout to passenger traffic on 15 June 1964, a number of isolated sections being retained mainly for colliery working. On the penultimate day of operation, 12 June 1964, '57xx' class 0-6-0PT No 3717 is seen on the approach to Quakers Yard tunnel after leaving Penrhiwceiber with a Pontypool Road service. Having been absorbed by the GWR in February 1865, this became its busiest line across South Wales until 1922. During World War I 11,500 special coal trains were routed via Pontypool Road, whilst in World War II a booklet, issued to the German Luftwaffe in 1940, pictured Crumlin Viaduct showing its continuing strategic importance.

Above: Amongst a number of towns deprived of their rail links is the county town of Brecon, once possessing services to Neath, Merthyr, Hereford and Newport. Illustrated here on the Neath service '57xx' class 0-6-0PT No 4621 awaits departure on a sunny 23 June 1962. The imposing station building was once the headquarters of GWR constituent the Brecon & Merthyr Railway, and was built in 1871. *Alan Jarvis*

Talybont-on-Usk station was situated at the foot of the notorious seven mile, 1 in 38 climb to Torpantau summit on the line from Brecon to Merthyr, this being considered one of the most severe gradients in the country. A regular type for the line, '2251' class 0-6-0 No 2247, is shown on 7 July 1962 just having left the station, and about to cross an Usk tributary, with a Newport working. A serious accident occurred in December 1878, when a banked northbound goods consisting of 36 wagons and brakevan hauled by two locomotives, ran away due to a failure to pin down brakes at Torpantau. As the train accelerated the locos — now in reverse gear — began disintegrating and towards the bank's bottom left the rails, killing the majority of the crew. Complete closure came on 4 May 1964, Talybont station now being a local authority outdoor pursuits centre, whilst Pant to Torpantau has partly reopened as the 2ft gauge Brecon Mountain Railway. *Alan Jarvis*

In an especially scenic section of line, alongside the River Wye, 'Ivatt' class 2MT 2-6-0 No 46515 is shown with a Moat Lane to Brecon train between Builth Road and Builth Wells on 25 April 1962. From the early 1950s, these LMS designed locos superseded, amongst others, the 'Dean Goods' and 'Cambrian' Class 15 0-6-0s previously operated, becoming the mainstay of most services on this section of the former Cambrian system and elsewhere. Two of the engines associated with these lines are now preserved; No 46512 on the Strathspey Railway in Scotland and No 46521 on the SVR at Bridgnorth. *T.B. Owen*

Below: On that section of main line between Swansea and Port Talbot, '81xx' class 2-6-2T No 8102 approaches the western end of Neath (General) station with a coal train on 17 October 1962. The '81xx' series were only ten in number, being rebuilt from the '51xx', previously '31xx' class, commencing 1938, to a higher boiler pressure and with 5ft 6in driving wheels, resulting in greater tractive effort. *John Wiltshire*

Right: Although not strictly part of the old Great Western system, the former LMSR, previously LNWR, Central Wales line latterly came under the jurisdiction of the Western Region. The opportunity has therefore been taken to include this view, taken along the section closed to passengers on 13 August 1965, between Swansea (Victoria) and Pontardulais on 15 June 1964. Seen here '57xx' class 0-6-0PT No 4676 passes the site

of NCB Brynlliw colliery with a loaded coal train, probably originating from this point or NCB Gorseinon colliery. It will be noted that the former down line is already lifted. The train is heading towards the junction station at Pontardulais, where passenger workings from Shrewsbury now continue forward to Llanelly, reversing here to reach Swansea via the GWR main line from Carmarthen.

Left: Llangadog station, situated on the Central Wales line between Craven Arms and Swansea, was on that section of line between Llandovery and Llandilo, once jointly owned by the GWR and London Midland & Scottish Railway (LMSR). On a beautifully clear Spring day '57xx' class 0-6-0PT No 3678 is seen passing through with a freight from the Llandovery direction on 31 May 1963. *John Wiltshire*

Above: One of the more remote branches on the GWR system was that from Whitland to Cardigan, in the county of Pembroke in West Wales. Serving a mainly agricultural area, its original purpose was to provide access to the lead mine at Llanfyrnach and Glogue slate quarry. In view of its isolated situation it inevitably became a candidate for early withdrawal of services,

with closure to passengers taking effect on 10 September 1962. Freight traffic lingered on for a further eight months, finishing on 27 May 1963. In this study, a few weeks before passenger closure, '45xx' class 2-6-2T No 4557 prepares to run round its train at the terminus before returning to Whitland on 16 June 1962. *Alan Jarvis*

A further view along the Cardigan branch, taken on the same day as the previous view, showing '16xx' class 0-6-0PT No 1648 with its single coach for Whitland, crossing the northbound service at Llanglydwen with an evening train. The local coal merchant's lorry will be observed, presumably waiting to unload the contents of the single BR 16-ton mineral wagon located in the siding. Judging by the film of rust on its rails, this had seen little use recently. On monthly market days, prior to World War II, a cattle, horse and sheep fair was held in the village for which a special train was normally run from Carmarthen. This would be invariably hauled by a 'Dean Goods' 0-6-0, the only tender type to work over the branch. The '16xx' class, introduced in BR days in 1949, had been constructed as a lightweight replacement for similar tanks of the '1901' and '2021' classes which had become due for withdrawal. With the rundown of the duties for which they were designed they had relatively short lives, No 1659 lasting only five years in service. *Alan Jarvis*

A spotless 'Manor' class 4-6-0 No 7802 *Bradley Manor* departs Machynlleth on 26 September 1964 with the Aberystwyth portion of the down 'Cambrian Coast Express'. Aberystwyth depot, then under the control of shedmaster Danny Rowlands, was noted for the excellent turn out of the engines provided for this prestige working. During 1963 the London Midland Region (LMR) assumed responsibility for the former Cambrian main line, and with the withdrawal of the last 'Manors' in 1965, the Standard Class 4MT 4-6-0s took over services. Cleaning declined, and a shabby No 75021 hauled the last down service on 4 March 1967.

Left: BR Standard Class 4MT 4-6-0 No 75004, in passably clean condition, leaves Towyn on 26 September 1964 with a short freight. A gunpowder van from the explosives factory at Penrhyndeudraeth is visible in the middle of the consist. Towyn is noteworthy as the headquarters of the independent narrow gauge Talyllyn Railway.

Above: Running alongside the River Wnion Ivatt Class 2MT 2-6-0 No 46520 carries out a shunting movement at Dolgelly on 28 November 1964, with the stock of a short working from Barmouth, and is presumably stabling prior to the return journey. This section of the Ruabon line from Barmouth was originally Cambrian Railway territory, and formed an end-on junction with the GWR line. The Cambrian had originally planned a separate terminus, the rails not meeting at the Bala & Dolgelly Railway station some distance away. A deviation was eventually built to allow a junction, and opening took place on 21 June 1869. The line closed throughout, after flood damage, on 18 January 1965.

A Birkenhead to Paddington express, headed by 'King' class 4-6-0 No 6001 *King Edward VII* tackles Saunderton summit, near Princes Risborough, with its eleven coach train on 17 March 1962. Dieselisation had by this time made considerable impact on Western Region main lines, the Birmingham route being the last to use these famous engines on a regular basis. Later in the year diesel power took over completely, the remaining six locomotives being retained on standby until the close of 1962. Apart from nationally preserved No 6000 *King George V*, Nos 6023 and 6024 have also survived, both based at Didcot. *T.B. Owen*

Princes Risborough situated on the GWR/GCR joint line from Paddington and Marylebone and on the direct route to Birmingham, was also the junction for the joint branch to Aylesbury. '14xx' class 0-4-2T No 1473 is shown with the branch service on 27 August 1960. Just over seven miles long, the line originally boasted three intermediate stations, one of these, South Aylesbury Halt, closing in June 1967. The branch is still served by through trains from Marylebone. *Roy Denison*

Left: The opening of the GWR line to Aynho Junction, which was extended from the GWR/GCR joint route at Ashendon Junction, reduced the Paddington to Birmingham distance by some 19 miles compared with the previous routeing via Oxford, and was also some two miles shorter than the LNWR route via Rugby. Known as the Aynho cut-off its construction involved considerable heavy engineering, with up and down lines carried through the Chiltern Hills on split levels in deep chalk cuttings. Opening to goods traffic was on 4 April 1910 and to passengers on 1 July 1910. At

Aynho connection was made with the original route to London via Oxford and Reading, and illustrated here we see 'Modified Hall' class 4-6-0 No 7918 *Rhose Wood Hall* heading south with a Birmingham to Hastings and Eastbourne working on 7 July 1962. On arrival at Reading this train would probably take the Southern Region line to Redhill following an engine change. Certain summer trains were worked throughout to Redhill by Western Region engines and men, '43xx' and 'Manor' classes being permitted over these metals. *T.B. Owen*

Above: This interesting view, taken from an overbridge, shows the unusual junction station of Swan Village on the Wolverhampton to Birmingham line, AEC powered railcar W8W having arrived with the 3pm Dudley to Birmingham (Snow Hill) on 1 June 1957. The railcar, built 1936, is one of the original streamlined series, a total of 18 being constructed mainly by the Gloucester Railway Carriage & Wagon Co. A further 20, built at Swindon, were added in 1940/1, these having a more angular appearance. *John Edgington*

73

Wednesbury Central, between Birmingham and Wolverhampton, is the location of this view showing '72xx' class 2-8-2T No 7228 with an up freight working on 28 May 1960. The route is now part of the Midland Metro system. The '72xx' series were reconstructed from '5205' and '42xx' class 2-8-0Ts, as a replacement for elderly 'Aberdare' class 2-6-0s due for withdrawal. Fifty four examples were ultimately rebuilt from 1934 to 1939, and three, Nos 7200, 7202 and 7229, have survived into preservation. They can be found at Quainton Road, Didcot and Bury respectively, though none is currently restored. *R.C. Riley*

Oakengates, east of Wellington and on the main line between Shrewsbury and Wolverhampton, is featured here with 'Hall' class 4-6-0 No 5917 *Westminster Hall* approaching Oakengates tunnel on an unidentified up express on 18 August 1962. The over 13 miles section from Shrewsbury, initially broad gauge, was completed in ten months on 1 June 1849. Boring of the 471yd tunnel presented a particular difficulty, the navvies having to work 24 hours continuously in unseasonable weather, to ensure completion to Wolverhampton in an acceptable time. This was reached on 12 November 1849, six weeks behind schedule. *T.B. Owen*

Left: Distinctive engines associated with the old Cambrian Railway system for many years, were the '90xx', formerly '32xx', series of 4-4-0s, commonly known latterly by the description 'Dukedogs'. This arose from their construction, being a combination of 'Duke of Cornwall' type boiler with a withdrawn 'Bulldog' frame. Despite their antiquated appearance they were comparatively modern being rebuilt between 1936 and 1939. The prototype, 'Duke' class 4-4-0

No 3265 *Tre Pol & Pen*, was itself rebuilt in 1930, the general weakness of 'Duke' frames having provided the catalyst. Illustrated here is No 9012 on the 2.05pm Whitchurch to Welshpool taking water at Oswestry on 6 April 1955. Originally allocated the names of Earls, all were later transferred to 'Castle' class 4-6-0s. However, No 9017 survived long enough to be preserved, and can be seen on the Bluebell Railway as No 3217 *Earl of Berkeley*. *John Edgington*

Above: Seen here is 'Ivatt' class 2MT 2-6-0 No 46512 and train shortly after leaving Bryngwyn Halt on the final stage of its journey to Llanfyllin on 27 November 1964. This branch was opened from Llanymynech on 10 April 1863 by the Oswestry & Newtown Railway. During the 1880s it saw a considerable increase in all traffic, due to use as a railhead for the building of the Vyrnwy Reservoir. No 46512 survives on the Strathspey Railway at Aviemore.

77

Above: On an early autumn morning 'Ivatt' class 2MT 2-6-0 No 46514 arrives at Fenns Bank with a Whitchurch to Oswestry working on 27 November 1964. This line was completed on 27 July 1864, the initial stretch of nearly 11 miles between Whitchurch and Ellesmere opening to all traffic on 4 May 1863. This involved the crossing of Fenns Moss, requiring employment of a timber-framed brushwood raft as part of the foundations. Similar difficulties were encountered on the 7-miles section between Ellesmere and Oswestry, where a further peat bog had to be crossed. The first section was worked initially by the LNWR, until the merger of the various independent railways forming the Cambrian system on 25 July 1864. Of note is the grounded carriage body providing additional station facilities, and the redundant pallet vans stored in various sidings. These were notorious for derailment at speed, due to their short wheelbase.

Right: An unidentified BR Standard Class 5MT 4-6-0 crosses the Dee Viaduct on the main line south of Ruabon, with a southbound passenger working on 28 November 1964. The line between Chester and Shrewsbury was completed on 12 October 1848, a special opening train of 59 carriages hauled by three locomotives, conveying local dignitaries to Shrewsbury. The 19 span viaduct built predominantly in stone stands 147ft high and is over 1500ft in length.

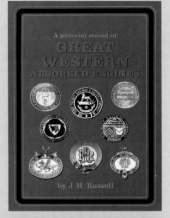